Aliyah

Battle Rattle Press
www.BattleRattlePress.com

Wish you Were Here!

ALIYAH

Aliyah is the immigration of Jews from the diaspora to, historically, the geographical Land of Israel, which is in the modern era chiefly represented by the State of Israel. Traditionally described as "the act of going up", moving to the Land of Israel or "making aliyah" is one of the most basic tenets of Zionism.

Zionist ideology was premised upon the reconstitution of the Jews as a free, self-determining nation in their own state. In recognition of this aspiration, Israel's Declaration of Independence declared that "The State of Israel will be open to the immigration of Jews and for the ingathering of exiles from all countries of their dispersion." In 1950, this principle was given shape as the Law of Return, enshrining this Zionist principle within Israeli law. The Law of Return grants every Jew in the world the automatic right to immigrate to Israel – in Hebrew called aliyah – and immediately become a citizen of the state.

The Law of Return did not arise from ideology alone; it was also a practical measure. In the wake of the Holocaust, the first act of the new Israeli government was to abolish all restrictions on Jewish immigration. Israel, the government declared, would provide Jews the world over with a haven from anti-Semitism.

Facing Page: Author/Poet David ben Levi atop Masada, 2017

Aliyah
Battle Rattle Press
London, Ontario
Published in Canada 2022
ISBN: 978-1-7781321-2-4

Copyright 2022

"You are shaking… so am I.
It is because of Jerusalem, isn't it?
One does not go to Jerusalem,
one returns to it.

That's one of its mysteries."

- Elie Wiesel

Legacy

I was conceived in the madness
of love in madness.
Endowed with the genes of despair
and the frailty of hope.

Born with a scarred soul,
an inheritance of pain,
a legacy of tears.

My crib sat in the shadow
of empty cribs.

My laughter, evoked tears of loss.
My joy, brought distanced silence.

Childhood friends were ghosts
of those who were
and would have been.

Bedtime stories
filled my dreams
with breaking glass.

I slept with nameless spirits,
and woke to dreams of Zion.

They are gone,
but we share a shadow.
For I am who they were
and they are who I am.
And Israel
with her dowry of hope
has welcomed us both.

Aliyah

I read the book
I camp on every word.
I hear the songs
that I have never heard.
I look at things
that I have never seen.
And I return
to where I've never been.

The songs of Zion
comfort, give me rest.
For Abrams' heart
beats within my breast.
The hills, the stones, the roses
there I find.
When I return
in the Aliyah of my mind.

"In Israel, in order to be a realist you must believe in miracles."

- David Ben-Gurion

Too Young

I was born in 1967.
I am too young to know
that you can get to hell
on a railway car.

I cannot know
what it is like
To see Dante's Inferno,
jackbooted
coming down my street.

Fright

The darkness gone,
the doorway bright.

Ahead the sun,
behind, the night.

A prayer for peace,
yet cursed to fight.

A family, friends,
and festive light.

A common home,
a mutual right.

Dreams for all,
within my sight.

I have no wish,
to use my might.

If only you
didn't want the night.

Sabra

sa·bra / ˈsäbrə/

An Israeli born in the land of Israel, in contrast to one who has immigrated.

In Hebrew, the word Sabra also refers to the prickly fruit of a species of cactus.

Sabras compare themselves to the fruit, which "has a prickly exterior and a soft interior."

The sun
sets over Samaria.

And just beyond
the window
Kinneret glistens
and rolls.

Passions awoken.

Jasmine and cordite
in her hair
incense my soul.

And always...
sand in the sheets
at the foot of the bed.

Her hold
her scratches
her storm
runs deep.

Our Galils stand together
in the corner,

empty wine glasses
on the window sill,

the Torah on the nightstand.

Passions softened.
The morning sun of Judea
streams through the lace,
crosses coffee arms
and warms vanilla breasts.
She wakes.

My sabra.

*"Never shall I forget that night,
the first night in camp,
that turned my life into one long night seven times sealed.
Never shall I forget that smoke.
Never shall I forget the small faces
of the children whose bodies I saw transformed into smoke
under a silent sky.
Never shall I forget those flames that consumed my faith forever."*

- Elie Wiesel, on his first night in Auschwitz.
He was 15 years old when he and his family were deported to the camp in May 1944.

Never See

My children,
Sing the songs of Zion
Sing them proud and free.
If you must sing
from on a watchtower
then so let it be.

Sing with power
sing with praise
sing to G-d with me.
Israel's sand, we're in our land,
Babylon, you'll never see.

My children
pray the prayers of Zion,
pray them strong and true.
Let them see
we will be free
we'll do what we must do.

Pray with power
pray with praise
pray to G-d with me.
Israels sand, we're in our land,
Masada, you'll never see.

"In Israel, free men and women are every day demonstrating the power of courage and faith.

Back in 1948, when Isreal was founded, pundits claimed the new country could never survive.

Today, no one questions that.

Israel is a land of stability and democracy in a region of tyranny and unrest."

- Ronald Reagan

Where Are the Prophets?

The rocks and the swords
are bleached in the sun.
The sickle and ploughshares
are beat into guns.

The Torah not read
the Talmud not told.
Where oh where
are the prophets of old?

Where is Nehemiah
as he stood on the wall?
And David, and Micah,
and Nahum and all?

Like a bird in the night
flying from dawn,
the Ark, the temple,
the prophets are gone.

No man in the tower,
no voice in the street,
no light to our path,
no lamp to our feet.

Our hearts and our eyes,
are dry as the sand,
until we return
to more than the land.

Amos 9:14-15

14 I will restore the fortunes of my people Israel, and they shall rebuild the ruined cities and inhabit them; they shall plant vineyards and drink their wine, and they shall make gardens and eat their fruit.

15 I will plant them on their land, and they shall never again be uprooted out of the land that I have given them," says the Lord your G-d.

I see that the darkness
always returns.

I see that the promise
withers and burns.

I see that the hatred
seems to prevail.

I see that goodness
is destined to fail.

I light the light
and hope that I'm wrong.

I light the light
and search for a song.

I light the light
in the depths of despair.

I light the light
without even a prayer.

Light Rail

Waiting for the Jerusalem Light Rail
on the platform across the street
from Damascus Gate.
I stand beguiled
by the vibrant potpourri
of what is Israel.

A half dozen young people
standing separately
olive drab uniforms
weapons slung
over their shoulders.
Each one with their faces
buried deep
in their cell phones.
Except for the one young man
with the scriptures
where his cell phone
apparently should be.

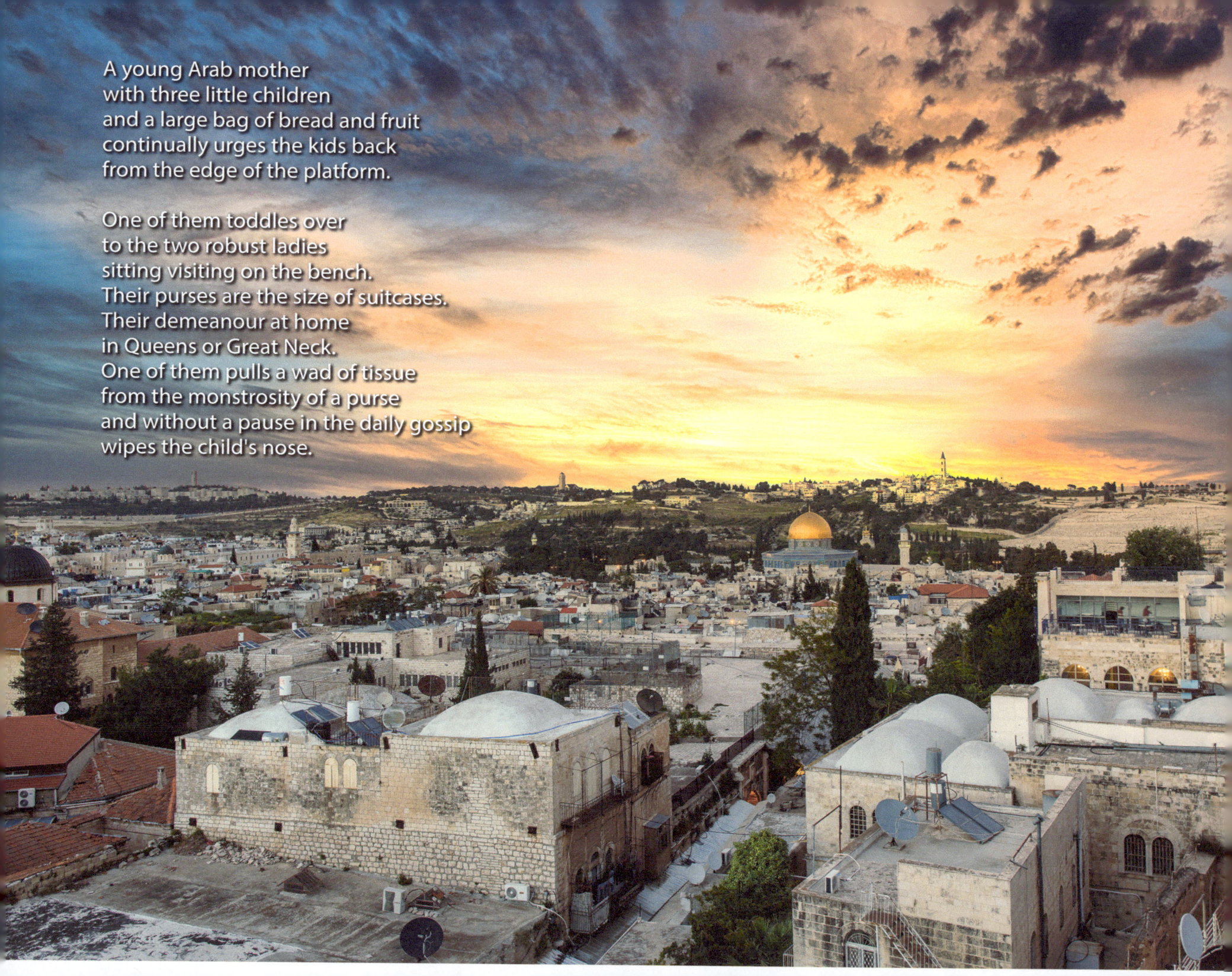

A young Arab mother
with three little children
and a large bag of bread and fruit
continually urges the kids back
from the edge of the platform.

One of them toddles over
to the two robust ladies
sitting visiting on the bench.
Their purses are the size of suitcases.
Their demeanour at home
in Queens or Great Neck.
One of them pulls a wad of tissue
from the monstrosity of a purse
and without a pause in the daily gossip
wipes the child's nose.

A few more travellers
Join the little group assembled.

Two Filipino Catholic monks
In long brown robes.

A tourist couple, both in cowboy hats,
are drinking cokes
and talking very loudly.

A very large and bulging man
with hairy arms and hairy tummy
which hangs below
his sweaty shirt
carries ka'ak bread rings
covered in sesame
in each hand
which he alternates as he bites.

A young Haredi man
rocks quietly
like the flame of a candle
while he reads and prays.

And a tall, and very thin
young black teen
wears massive earphones
which cradle his kippah.
His music blasts.
The fringes of his Tzitzit
hang from the corners
and appear from under
his vintage Van Halen t-shirt.

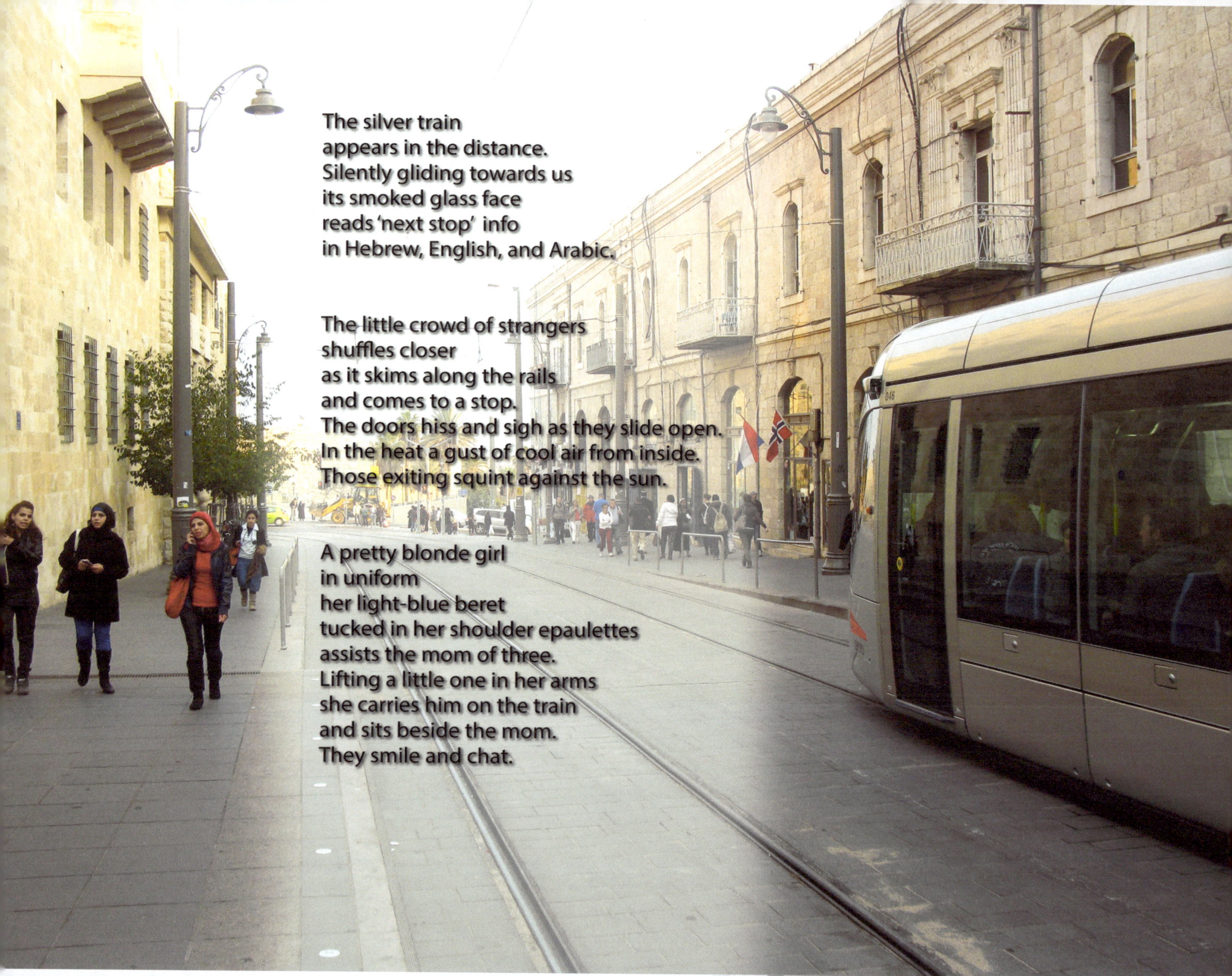

The silver train
appears in the distance.
Silently gliding towards us
its smoked glass face
reads 'next stop' info
in Hebrew, English, and Arabic.

The little crowd of strangers
shuffles closer
as it skims along the rails
and comes to a stop.
The doors hiss and sigh as they slide open.
In the heat a gust of cool air from inside.
Those exiting squint against the sun.

A pretty blonde girl
in uniform
her light-blue beret
tucked in her shoulder epaulettes
assists the mom of three.
Lifting a little one in her arms
she carries him on the train
and sits beside the mom.
They smile and chat.

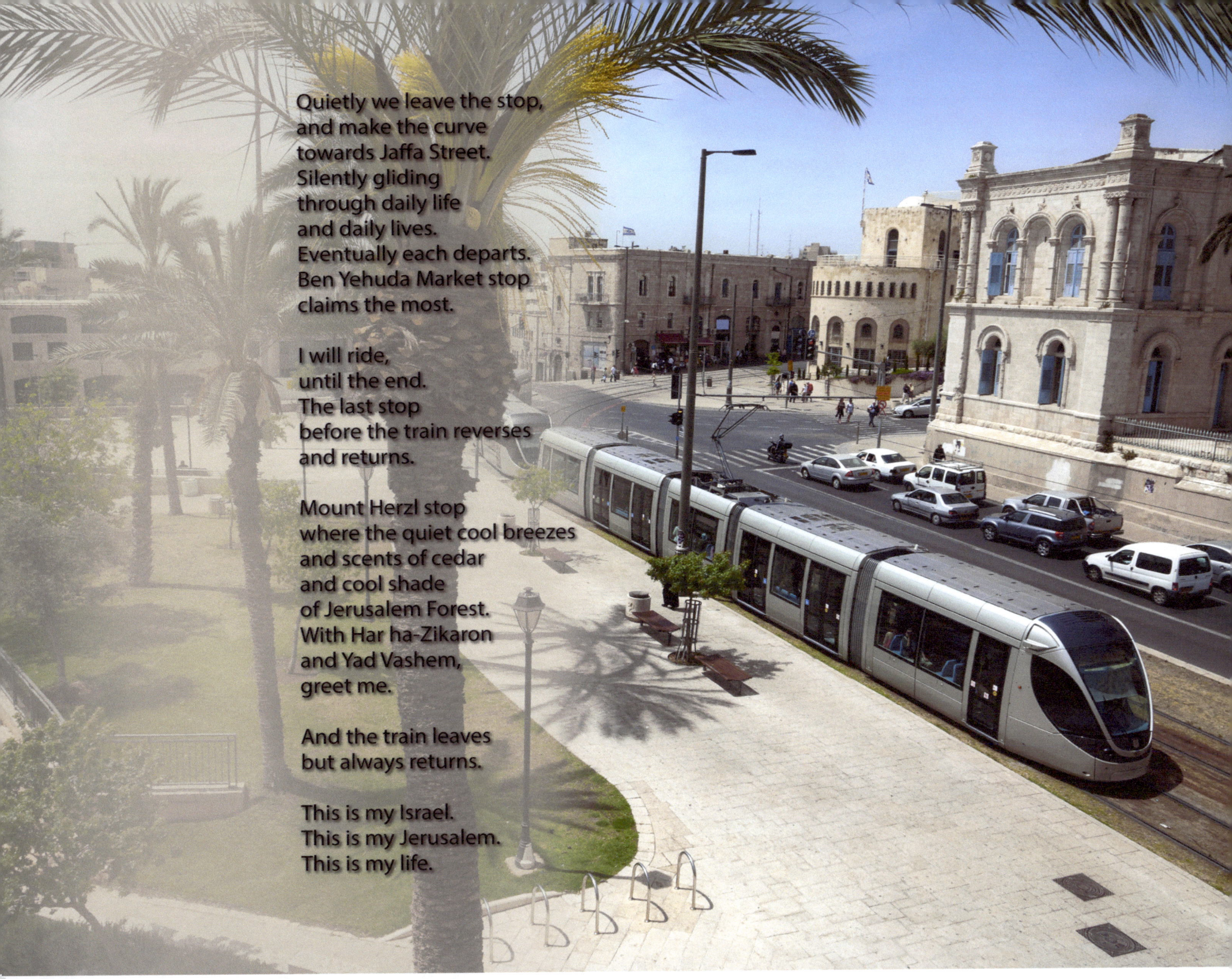

Quietly we leave the stop,
and make the curve
towards Jaffa Street.
Silently gliding
through daily life
and daily lives.
Eventually each departs.
Ben Yehuda Market stop
claims the most.

I will ride,
until the end.
The last stop
before the train reverses
and returns.

Mount Herzl stop
where the quiet cool breezes
and scents of cedar
and cool shade
of Jerusalem Forest.
With Har ha-Zikaron
and Yad Vashem,
greet me.

And the train leaves
but always returns.

This is my Israel.
This is my Jerusalem.
This is my life.

Odette to a Pomegranate

Oh humble pomegranate
so delectable and sweet
Why do you make your goodness
so difficult to eat?

Do I pick each seed alone
Feel it burst with juice so sweet
Do I scoop it with a spoon
An ambrosial joy to eat

Were you there within the garden?
Was it you that tempted Eve?
Is your blood red syrup streaming
Throughout much that I believe.

When the twelve allied in silence
And went out to spy the land
They returned with pomegranates
And they helped us understand.

Your fruit it stands for wisdom
And has just so many seeds,
Each one for a mitzvot
Of the Torah, as it reads.

I could sing about your sweetness
Of your hope throughout our flight,
Of your celebration promise
For prosperity and light.

But for now I'll take a moment
To retreat for daily strife.
Relax, recharge,
get off my feet,
while you refresh my life

About the Author

David benLevi is the poetic pseudonym of author, poet, artist, retired Lieutenant-Commander David Lewis.

David served in the US Army during the cold war in the 1980s stationed in West Germany and spent much of the early 1990s working in humanitarian aid for the former Soviet Union, and then the bulk of the 2000's in the Royal Canadian Navy on various operations which included a tour in Afghanistan in 2011-12. Among his numerous military service awards and decorations are the General Campaign Star – South-West Asia, Meritorious Service Medal, Commander Canadian Army Commendation, and others.

While his poetry tends to be more Israel-centric, his artworks (oil, watercolour, pastel and graphite) tend to be more historic military, first responder or holocaust based. An avid writer, he tends to write from personal experience or current or human events.

To stay out of trouble during his recent retirement he began www.BattleRattleCandleCompany.com in which he creates military, or Israel scented candles.

He has also created www.BattleRattlePress.com in which he endeavours to help other veterans and first responders find their voice and tell their story.

www.ingramcontent.com/pod-product-compliance
Lightning Source LLC
Chambersburg PA
CBHW042129200426

43209CB00064B/1865